DEATH
EGG

DEATH EGG

poetry by
Nathaniel Duggan

published by
back patio press
2023

We encourage photographing, posting, sharing, and otherwise broadly disseminating excerpts from this book for promotional, educational, and review purposes. We only ask for full attribution to the author.

This is a work of fiction. Nothing is real.

ISBN: 979-8-9887637-0-3

Cover and typesetting by Zac Smith
Published by Back Patio Press
backpatiopress.com / backpatio.press

CONTENTS

DEATH EGG

LIKE A DOG RETURNING TO VOMIT

I am going to destroy myself
so hard today
with juggled chainsaws
and torches imbibed
orally. I will annihilate
the entire nation of me
with a nuclear bomb
unless demands are met.
I am a bug in violent August
whose shell has burst.
I have lost track
of the days of my bender.
I am going to confuse
the part for its whole,
the scrambling ants
for the hill they refuse
to die on.

GIANT SQUID POEM

Year of excellent back-to-school specials,
of giant squids smashing oil tankers:
Year of the Rat. No one remembers
their phone number.
The coasts are stained with ink
and high school dropouts.
When the giant squid plummets ashore,
it is transparent as an uncle's drug habit,
its eyes gashes. *How terrifying,*
everyone concedes,
gathering their Piña Coladas,
going back to work.
I linger past nightfall
in the fantasy where the squid
is my CGI Disney companion. It only rots
a little, and I measure the ocean
by how deep the moon sinks.

THE UNIVERSE IS A GIANT UNFEELING ROBOT PART 1

A small town that digests you.
Rain falling up. The martyr
whose death is reversed
like a tragic Uno Card.
Sometimes there are too many throats,
tomorrow is Pizza Day,
the big bang never happened,
and light and governments expand
outward but sadness is
more like a particle
than a wave—you've got
your crying backwards.

TEENAGE SWAMP CREATURE MISERY

This was a January unlike any before it.
Everyone everywhere suffered
and other people's pain
meant nothing to me.
My wife claimed time was a construct
during the divorce proceedings.
I was a spectral being
perceptible only in mirrors
and the gene-edited selection
of TV soap operas,
drunk before noon,
trespassing in the dead malls
of an empty everything.
How could eye contact happen
in these circumstances?
How could I ever swear to kill you,
my treasonous brother?
In your fingerprints alone
there are a hundred billion people

all sheepish and failing to find love
in grocery store parking lots.

ATOMIC BOMB POEM

Baby come on over I have
an unlimited capacity for failure
I have a cyborg heart constructed
from Honda Civic cupholders I have
a 40oz of malt liquor this night can't
end I haven't used my Sam's Club
Membership yet it gets too dark too quick
this close to the sky so close and still
you can't touch it just like the space
they say exists between every atom
baby come on over I have
never once been touched

DIRECTIONS TO VACATIONLAND

Kill me in a national park
because my heart is 3 to 5
unpaid parking tickets
and sometimes I fall in love
with my best friend's little sisters.
But forget the gerrymandered prom.
Regret nothing, regret is nothing
but a short scuttle, there and back,
through the business districts
of Japanese armpit pornography.
My clone films a blockbuster there
in which he assassinates me,
from behind, with a coconut.
That's heaven alright. What else
can I say looking like next week's
supervillain, spliced as I am now
into so many lost hangovers.

SHARK WEEK

Either I've run out of things to conquer
or they've all run away from me.
Perhaps I am not fit for murky water.
I am a cruel governor craving
tropical getaways, solutions clear
as a boiled ocean. Most of all I want
to box the shark with hammers for brains
to death in a seafloor cage.
Nowadays everything I police scatters
to plankton, outnumbering the stars.
Nowadays I fight the skin cells
I lose each night, tiny aboriginals
shoving me out of bed, shadows
making puppets of my meaty gestures.

INSECT MIMICRY

Beetles feign a poison
they lack. She left me
over the drinking. 'Mocktail' sounds
like a kind of ancient scorpion unearthed.
I arrive at weddings uninvited,
I walk at wayward angles,
I will appear alarming to you
and talk too loudly about politics
until you go away
and I will have an excuse
for everything I do not have.

X-PARASITE

Assume all living organisms
have been replaced. I am not
a symptom of anything. Dousing
cigarettes in a swimming pool.
Taking a bath in a suit. Sometimes
I have these inscrutable panics:
microwaved fish,
missed calls from mom,
the annual family barbeque. Theoretically,
it is impossible to explain
my oven-mitted sobbing,
these convenience store heartbreaks.
This doesn't suck.
I am so happy.

A SINGLE DAY OF MY LIFE WOULD VANQUISH ONE HUNDRED ARMIES

People make outrageous claims.
The salesmen parade
a new kind of grief,
one collapsible, with a tarp
in case of rain. These shiny
objects will vanish in time,
history is over,
the sky breaks
beneath the angels attacking,
surrogate endpoint
of a diner in Ohio,
Tuesday morning,
all is lost
but the salt on your eggs.

CLOSE THE SKY

and open the hatches
to the nuclear submarine
of your last hangover
in which you swore
never to kill again, samurai
with the wooden blade. Life
as the incremental process
of dulling yourself. Just a little something
to take the edge off: beer after work,
garden hose of whiskey,
the feudal betrayal
of your last lover spawning
a dozen centuries of darkness,
because we needed to outlaw heaven
and the part of each late afternoon
where there's a morsel of death
and the microwave dings blue.

PLACES TO ESCAPE

Arctic scientists discover
a new type of suicide,
contagious and sweeping.
I had lost interest in my own life,
breaking nightly into the psych ward
to rave about oversized dolls,
doors behind mirrors leading
to more doors. It can be hard
to distinguish between places
to escape and to infiltrate.
Sometimes you have to rob
your own grave. Sometimes
you eat around
the bone.

DEATH EGG

You want in your life
a doomsday device,
you want a city detonated.
Birds are softer lately.
We miss beer ads
and war. The bombs
don't go off, fast food ends
history, and the final egg
is the death egg,
fortress of loss
and takeout receipts,
conveyor of a destruction
so complete
it kills you backwards,
birthing you again
and again.

I'VE SEEN SO MUCH ASS ON THE INTERNET I'VE BECOME NUMB TO IT

grocery store fried chicken
potato chips for breakfast
I could tell that some part
of my heart had gone rotten
but I didn't feel like stopping

BLOOD BEAM

so many frivolous things in this world!
a super moon every month now
everything in the news sounding
like signature attacks
Bivalent Booster, Burst Wolf Claw
Dark Digivolution
learning a new beam attack
call it Blade Beam
the playground had a cutting wind to it
the rain lasted an entire recess
I slumped home
unmarked buoy of the soul
a car dealership in Missouri

KING KONG

for g.g. roland

at the zoo showing porn to the gorillas
on a half-moon of nausea somewhere
between prom and the next interstate
my hangover calling to say
it fucked your mother
feeling that 'I am the monkey'
we are all the monkey, maybe
inside everyone something rages
ideally it would be infinite and righteous
it would be King Kong dismantling Godzilla
it would be the cold blood shucked
from your junior high nemesis
not this hemorrhoid of dread
pachinko of shed skin
America is only exceptional in some regards

THE GREATEST SADNESS THAT CAN EVER BE EXPERIENCED IS ANYTIME AFTER MIDNIGHT IN A 7-11

Burnt tofu fractals
and no satisfaction in beer.
I die 1,000 deaths of despair
and it's not even Tuesday.
Mice lie, monkeys exaggerate.
Permanent insanity.
The horrible mass graves
of children. The empty Walmart parking lot
behind your face. We could end
loneliness by building robots,
we could run out of placebos,
we could have 25 micrograms
of ancestral strain,
the final antigenic sin,
a cupped breast
in the saddest back row
of a summer blockbuster.

TENTACLE PORN BLUES

I want out
of the unpaid internship
of the hole in my heart
shaped like an attic
drunk with bassoonists.
My body can do so little,
it is just a ratio
of salt and water,
a beach house party
no one invited me to.
Still I can't complain
when Tom Cruise
is the last samurai
dying of thirst
outside a strip mall.
By the time
my day off arrives
the city is bombed,
the endless war is over,
and I am all that's left
to be shushed
and shipwrecked

HAMSTER HEAVEN

There are no castles in America just
barbeques and biblically-accurate angels.
Dead animals raining down
from hamster heaven.
I cannot be created or destroyed.
My grief is a biblically-accurate Disneyland,
its spires wet cardboard,
its beer shaken as grenades.
I'm going to prove something incredible
killing the next person in line,
I will gun down so many minivan families
that my talking points escape me
like tiny pets thudding beneath
their dumb cemeteries.

DECODED TRANSMISSIONS FROM THE BILLION-POUND JELLYFISH

The bottom of the ocean is
a terrible place to go
blind. This sadness is
a millipede without legs.
This sadness weighs
a billion pounds and will
last longer than plastic.
Like an alien mothership,
like a floating continent
of garbage, it cannot be
detected by radar,
it will not biodegrade.
Call this an evolutionary
advantage: biological
immortality.
If you keep yourself
a sponge, you can never
truly be crushed.

VARIANT

Someone on a podcast defines
'harm' as 'tissue damage
to the body'. It will never go away.
It just hides for a while
beneath your bed, 100-year
hibernation of cicadas.
I brood. I bomb a hospital
and bicker with you
over nothing, really.
Now I have to burn
everything I've achieved,
and you mistake my collapse
for just another beachside condo.

INCREASINGLY I FEEL I HAVE ABSOLUTELY NOTHING TO SAY TO ANYONE WHO DOES NOT DISPLAY INTEREST IN SPEEDRUNS OF THE VIDEO GAME METROID OR THE ROLE PRIVATE EQUITY HAS PLAYED IN DESTROYING MODERN RETAIL

Brittle-blue skies in late autumn
remind me of failing relationships
and the first level of *Metroid Prime*,
the Chozo Ruins. I look best
emaciated. All my poems start
with 'me.' Every single one of my defeats
is tactical, such as this second puke

of the day. I lost something vital
that summer in the Taco Bell drive-thru,
ever since I've been mugged nightly
in the shadows of a city that has no name.
If tomorrow is a crushed beer can
then the world is a shape
that should've been made
to fit me.

DISQUALIFIED AS A HUMAN BEING

When you know you are a false prophet,
failure can cling to you like cotton candy,
like fiberglass on the tongue. Luckily
your scars look as lovely as moons.
Although everything looks like a moon
these days, which is to say cratered,
and somewhere within your wound you kiss
your sister by accident, you irradiate
the baby, and the collapsed telephone poles
of your suburb suddenly resemble
a spine's protrusion. The sun's angle
is entirely wrong. The angel's wings
melt. In the remains of an hour,
you order your lunch to go.

RENT-A-KILL

They could use some taxes around here,
they could deliver death
by firing squad. In the meantime
I wear shorts colorful
as reptile poison. I'm figuring out
the foreign policy of your blues.
Because there is always a practical solution,
always a hero arriving late,
there is a law firm
right beside the rusty laundromat
named 'Rent-a-Kill'
specializing
in personal injury.
I show up to the office far too late
still wearing my vivid shorts,
the fly undone.

THOSE YOUNG MEN WHO LIKED TO IMAGINE THEIR HEARTS AS ANCHORS ARE NOW OLD

it's called a 'boom'
because of the sound it makes
when it concusses your father's skull
flinging him overboard
and you are left
on his ship you cannot sail
fisted by a wind
you can no longer hear
the waves like one billion palms
all opening in 'hello!'

MY DOWNFALL IS A BACKROOM DEAL

I want my sadness to dissipate
perfectly, like in a haiku,
hot rain on summer pavement,
etc,
but lately it's more like atomic breath,
a mutagen lizard whose tail will not stop
regrowing, it has sixteen heads
all terminal with cancer.
So I take up hobbies, investing,
sabotaging US presidencies,
a stock market of shed skin:
doctors recommend losing
enough of yourself
to create an evil twin
on which to pin your crimes.
Now I'm learned in the supply and demand
of pedestrian hurts, and the sale
of my liver goes unregulated,
my grievances vanish in the black night
of supermarket saving secrets.

SUPER METROID

pretending my hangover
is an ever-deepening space cavern
I can get a little melodramatic
on Margarita Mondays
I am a spreadsheeted office worker
not a galactic bounty hunter exploring
the alien tunneled carpentry
of your last kiss
my headache not so bad
once I adjust for inflation

GALACTIC SPACE OPERA

My sister adopted a dog that had a bone tattoo.
Meaning, this puppy was 'bad to the bone'.
He chain-smoked cigarettes.
He shared unverified information
on social media.
I was glimpsed buying cocaine
from him in the back alley
of a biker bar named 'The Roost'
and subsequently banned
from every establishment.
This was the kind of dog
who catches the car and knows exactly
what to do with it,
which is more than I can say
for myself,
and I have caught
so many fucking cars.

DOOMSDAY PREPARATION

Because the horizon is
a supermassive dying angel,
and the sky will once again bloody
like tissue paper,
even in your bedroom ceiling's blankness
where there is no sky.
Somewhere buried beneath all this
stirs a tiny but battle-
starved beetle.
How quickly any place
can become your shell.

VASECTOMY CASTRATION MUTILATION CIRCUMCISION POEM

the smallest wire
within you gets snipped
the wrong bomb goes off
the city explodes
the cast of a 90s sitcom
engineers a police surveillance state
to canned laughter and applause
picking up a megaphone I urge
my people to become small
smaller than the grit beneath
their own fingernails
small enough to dodge atomic fission
small enough that I
don't have to see any of you
anymore

YOU VANQUISHED ME BUT HELL WAS FULL SO I CAME BACK TO KICK ASS AND DRINK BEER AND THERE IS PLENTY OF BEER, TOO MUCH MAYBE, I FEEL A LITTLE SICK AND TOMORROW I WILL BE HUNGOVER

Increasingly life seems like a thing
that just sort of happens. Thinking
about abandoning your family
as a non sequitur. Feeling irrevocably fucked
in a Wendy's. Asking for extra salt
on your fries. Wiping the salt from your fingers
with your tie. Life as automatic process,
an ugly hatching, a shot of vodka
prescribed by doctors. It becomes impossible
to distinguish reflex from consciousness,

the good rampaging kaiju from the bad,
your feet from your cowboy boots
as you stumble your longing out
in the tiny town with no moon.

LIGHT MISSILE

You'd been the victim
of a meaningless hope.
I was nostalgic for a grace
I'd never fallen from.
Now it's too late, the way
it always is, and we can't rule out
interplanetary bullshit,
this cosmic misfortune, this crow
at my birdfeeder. But no one
can chart the astrology
of the earth-destroying laser,
not one president can authorize
the ultimate missile,
and you remain forever out of range
of my beam attacks.

OBAMA 2.O

Mild brief insanity.
Nautilus-like extinct invertebrates
with 10-foot-long cone-shaped shells.
An octopus has 3 hearts and dies
giving birth. On the contrary,
no rose is born and everything
explodes, killer snails the size
of rats and there is no scenario
in which I am the villain,
I don't think of you anymore,
do you ever still think
about me, etc.

POLITICAL POEM

on a practical level, our nation lacks death
I am for anything that polls well
I have been trained by the US Secret Service
I have partied all night with horse tranquilizer
this town seeks to expose and humiliate me
I will appease my enemies at all costs
I will fold my spine in compromise
keeping my hopes moderated
and my love letters stamped
with anthrax kisses

EVIL CLONE POEM

I need more weapons within my reach
I am my own clone
it is a dilemma
because love is two assassins in a bowling alley
it is several henchmen pushing a button
I'm saying I have a table for two within me at all times
because I am both lonely and crowded
often the world is like something cruel and unnecessary
it should have been more like a gentle breeze
through a wind turbine executing birds

PERFECTLY ULTIMATE GREAT MOTH POEM

you had the best ass in a shady bar
I was activating my unlimited void technique
the desire to break the impossible cocoon of you
was like a state subsidized death ray
it was like the baristas unionizing
we emerged from ourselves shining but soggy
I liked you better telescoped
it was easier when you pieces of shit
were nothing but worms groveling before me

PRAYERS FOR MOTHRA

1.

instead of God
I worship
a shitty caterpillar

instead of work
I chug
a thousand shitty beers

like the Luna moth
I have no mouth
for all this hunger

eating myself up
the world's saddest
gas station pizza

2.

Imagine a huge moth. No,
even bigger.
Think planetary.
A bug heavier
than gravity,
its shadow vast
as a drone-bombed wedding,
its insect-heart alone
larger than your last divorce,
engorged as deep sea gigantism,
inner organs a mausoleum
for larvae yet unborn.
Ok.
Now breathe
because nothing is greater
than the tiniest parasite
in an intestine's lining,
and I am conquered yet again,
my day barely begun,
black iced coffee
on an empty stomach.

3.

Insects invade your garden,
a forbidden handjob wracks
the high school reunion.
The candidacy did not
pan out. We should ban
eye contact. Popular uprisings
make me uneasy—I don't like
crowds, their caterpillared gnawing.
The difference between moth
and butterfly remains sexual,
a certain angle of regret,
the way the light falls
from an open fridge
while you wonder
what's left to eat.

KING GHIDORAH LOVE POEM

That is to say my love is
a three-headed extraterrestrial
planet-killing dragon. It is a god
from another dimension.
It gets drunk at a small-town biker bar,
and its hangover is three actors
competing for control
of a complicated costume.
Clumsy with the morning,
knocking over trash bins,
I will grasp the gleaming scraps
of you and bury them
so completely
no star ever glitters again.

I HAVE TOO MANY MEMORIES OF BEING SAD AND WINDSWEPT IN A WALMART (I HAVE TOO MANY MEMORIES)

stumbling raggedly through the aisles of Walmart
feeling fucked in the hardware section
thinking, in the tone of a poetry collection,
'Places to Shit
in a Walmart'
feeling an abyssal horniness
a bottomless deep-sea lust
blind things swimming in it
thermal vents inhospitable to life exploding
oooooo yeah baby
orgasm of nuclear flashes
in submarine darkness
wanting to throatfuck the dentist
the dentist who has a practice at Walmart
for some reason

trying not to think about teeth
while fantasizing about throatfucking the dentist
and so imagining the opposite of teeth
the opposite of tooth is tongue
the opposite of grave is skin
missing the urinal
pissing a bit on your own leg
staining your pants with your hot piss
secreting yourself with you
people will think you've pissed yourself
in a Walmart
the cashier
the hot dentist
oh god
oh no
the righteous distinction
between pissing *inside* your pants
and a little bit of piss
spraying *onto* your pants
wanting life to be blank and pure
as Walmart's freshly mopped concrete
wanting to clone yourself
as easily as copying a set of keys
so that you can destroy yourself limitlessly
trying to sop up the piss with the automatic hand dryer
people walking in and staring
your leg propped on the sink

the dryer blowing
the island of piss on your pants, dark and brooding
dabbing at it with paper towels
your clone is out there somewhere, probably
like in that Arnold Schwarzenegger movie
your clone is out there fucking your wife
the person who would be your wife
if she wasn't getting fucked by your clone
the sound of a dryer in an empty bathroom
how excessive it seems
histrionic
a moonless howling
the piss mostly gone
alone with your Walmart reflection
you are the sale nobody asked for
but everyone is going to get
mass produced and heavily discounted
thinking about the opposite of emptiness
it's like a sucking, but in reverse
a hole that falls down you

IMMUNE ESCAPE

October's leukemia sky, instant ramen,
black coffee blues. A decisively distinct path
to democracy. A dead bird. That's the way
it always is with you: distant deserts,
small moons. I was born from an egg,
the death egg, and my sadness is a sickle
through cornfields. Cold woe, Kansas City:
lost space colony.
And the snow accumulates.
And I still love you. And if you try
to crush me, I will stick forever
to the bottom of your shoe.

IMPACT CRATER POEM

The stolen election came and went. I had
Gatorade for blood. You carried calamity
like a dead queen in your shirt pocket
and we were in love, grasshoppers
singing with chafed thighs
the lost Spanish of the town
built in a meteor impact's
echo. Winter of manmade stars.
Spring Toyotathon. I realized
nothing except the shadow clone
of your saddest Monday. The tiny wing
of your most murdered father. Together
we are like some great unclaimed tragedy,
and in jetports all over the world
the luggage continues to go missing.

IN A DIRECT FIGHT I WOULD CURL UP IN A BALL LIKE AN ARMADILLO, EXCEPT I DON'T HAVE A PROTECTIVE SHELL, SO YOU WOULD STILL END UP BEATING THE SHIT OUT OF ME

Don't be mean to me on Sundays.
Birds are omens, seagulls squabbling
over a Wendy's dumpster, dead crow
on highway shoulder picked apart
by other crows: you will leave me
politely, by appointment.
Likewise the firefighters
will not be held accountable.
The police unions break
for yet another lunch. Still,
if the future is a cracked egg,
why do swimsuit models smile
over their leggy calendars?

PEEING OFF SKYSCRAPERS

Mortally wounded from nowhere.
Gnats bring you down with tiny knives.
Once we've controlled for belief
polls show 46% 'very worried'
about extremist terrorism
and hotdogs ruined
by rained-in fairs.
Someone's had sex before,
the whales harpoon back lately,
and a hotel minifridge
is the loneliest space possible
per square foot in America.
Cathedral of the supermarket
frozen foods section,
that's what love will be like.

LOST MY JOB AGAIN AND SPENT 3 YEARS UNEMPLOYED, AS INTENDED

Thought 'America's eerie eternity'
crashing my 2009 Honda Civic at 15mph
in a 'The Matrix'-like slowness.
Mentally viewing myself as a supervillain
so I can pretend every loss is calculated.
The happiest moments of my life are
lying in bed with the lights off, not sleeping,
'biding my time'–
this room temperature misery
all part of the plan.

THE UNIVERSE IS A GIANT UNFEELING ROBOT PART 2

Horseshoe crab lunar spawning,
blood moon eclipse. The apocalypse
of another hangover. The routine
militarization of our first date.
I remember you by your gas station sushi,
and no one is forgetting the horror
of that day, the homicides spiking,
the failed colonial petro-state
of your right kidney, the heart
as generic steel, aluminum,
something you can crinkle
and wrap your lunch with,
foiled again.

HOCKEY PRACTICE

Likewise on the skating rink
of my scraped heart
abandoned orphans scrimmage out
another round of love and loss.
With each defeat they carve
a figure eight, scratch
tiny infinities until they beat
themselves blue and fall
into one another like towers,
like boxers whose collapse
is indistinguishable
from an embrace.

NATURE HAIKU FT. MATSUO BASHŌ

Having no talent
in a landlocked suburb
I mistake a leaf's scuttling
for a horseshoe crab.
Autumn gone. I am a clam
split in half down the road
from a wet t-shirt contest.
A cashier's breasts
blossom in the gas station.
Ice-sheathed beach,
even this late in winter,
crab shells smolder red.

THE FIRST VIRGIN ON THE MOON

When it snows I snowplow.
This may seem obvious at first
but it is the harsh crystallization
of an office shift tomorrow
and an online lover I lost.
When it snows I snowplow
and I feel like the Mars Rover
in all that blankness,
navigating a dusty planet,
pearl desert, my last transmission
chirped to no one's ears,
my last girlfriend named Liz–
send me to space
please, where I can be
the first virgin on the moon,
to where it does not snow.

PULLING THE WORLD APART WITH MY TEETH

Your last thought is a perilous one.
Another murder goes unsolved,
another planet is built
upon steel and suffering,
another Friday. Thank God
it's Friday. In a dead November
all that remains of any bug
is its shell, and everyone falls
asleep after the office pizza party,
drool pooling on their keyboards,
circuitry frying, the company stock
plunging. Your sadness is deep
as any crack in the ocean;
at its bottom gather
glow-in-the-dark squid.

LIFE INSURANCE

sad story: bought used car
in a fit of despair
from the shoe salesman
with a gun grafted to his arm
all that's given to us in this world
is artillery and excuses
now my geraniums bloom plastic
my horizons are spilled watercolors
every loss another Honda Civic
jumping over the moon

HEDGEHOG'S DILEMMA

People move through a city feeling
distinctly fake and fucked.
Somewhere a scientist has gone insane
and giant mutant mantises
soon destroy the world.
People shudder to think,
shutter their windows
and slug beer in darkness.
There has been some sort of mistake.
To what exactly do the mantises pray,
and how can you expect
to hold anyone tenderly
when your hands are blades.

PETRI DISH

Water laden with insects,
heavenly script of tadpoles burned
between your shoulders at the club.
I do drugs until my nose bleeds.
Scientists read the minds of jellyfish
because the merging of black holes
may swallow the universe.
The earth wants us murdered,
the mud wants you back,
and death is finally understood
obscurely, beneath a microscope,
cold winter star mistaken
for a firefly or just another winking
check engine light.

VOLTRON: LEGENDARY DEFENDER

Spend your days wandering the bars
like a private investigator removed from his case.
Even your pain has been appropriated
in a universe patrolled
by military-grade robots whose blueprints
resemble an insect's twitching.
Oysters go rotten on a beach
and not a single soul can police that.
Fine: let your palace be overrun
by ants.

BLACKWARGREYMON

In the very end
I was your ashes, virused twin
existing for the sake of a peculiar justice.
Meteor Wing, Positron Laser!!
I lost the house and kids.
I rewatched my childhood cartoons.
The heart's walls cannot be destroyed–
Gaia Force!!!!!!!
I remain impenetrable
to light and missiles
and to people, too.

APOCALYPSE POEM

A small sadness enters you
like a bat down a chimney.
Across the planet not one person
gets what she deserves.
Godzilla rages
in the last remaining city
and still the bored biologists
debate shark skeletons.
Still the kindest lunch ladies
give the worst haircuts
and what you mistook
for the sky's collapsing
was just another dusk.

ASTRONAUT ON AN UNSPECIFIED MISSION

You are the astronaut on an unspecified mission.
Wherever you are, it is already too late.
There are no more roads, lighthouses,
gas stations. Alone in your space motel
you drink 2 to 3 space beers. You cry a little
to space TV. All that is left
of your voyage is to chart the various
constellations in which you have been lost,
one final descent mapped
in dive bars, defunct satellites,
Martian deserts without air
or breeze where your footprints
may never sweep away.

UNTIL YESTERDAY, I THOUGHT MY LIFE COULD BE DIFFERENT, I WAS IN LOVE, ETC....

after Roberto Bolaño

Arrested yet again
by fake police
as sunlight falls
at weird hours
on an incoming comet
that punctures this sky
like fingers burrowing
down a missing girl's throat.
Some men will never be found.
Cops unpunished, joints
of a spine breaking against
themselves. Glass everywhere,
what I mean is sometimes
the agents in black suits go so
deep undercover
they forget who they are

or ever were, sometimes
you see yourself beaten to death
in a saloon's mirror,
and sometimes you are a slug
whose oozing reflects
everything you are not.

BASICALLY, EVERYONE SHOULD BE SUBORDINATE TO MY WISHES, BUT I NEVER WANT TO BE HELD RESPONSIBLE FOR ANYTHING EVER AGAIN

Outside the dusk and the bats fall
together. Somehow I am lost without
having ever left for anywhere.
The alien invaders have won,
nations toppled and battleships
set aflame. Oddly they look
harmless enough as they take
our capital, tiny crabs green
as coins not worth finding.

'KMART REALISM'-ESQUE SHORT STORY IDEA: I'M HUNGRY BUT GOING THROUGH A DIVORCE SO I DRIVE TO THE GAS STATION AND BUY CHIPS AND CHEESE DIP, THAT LIKE CHEESE-Y GLOBULAR DIP STUFF, AND I EAT ALONE IN MY CAR, AND THERE'S SMEARED CHEESE-Y HANDPRINTS AND FRACTALS OF NEON LIGHT EVERYWHERE

seems like the McRib is always
'back on the menu'
I can conceivably imagine
the last thought I ever have being
'back on the menu'
my car careening
into a highway guardrail

SAD LITTLE LOBSTER GURGLES

1.

Just as every snowflake melts alike
all these backroads look the same,
and I take a wrong turn into a lifetime
of selling mattresses. But I guess you can't
expect the whole ocean in one seashell.
I guess I don't know why you fear sleep
when you don't snore and you won't dream.
Me, I pass out at work, I wake too late—
late August, everyone fleeing their vacation,
and I lose you forever to bad traffic.
Already I forget my last nightmare,
something about a lobster chewing
the shell he just cast off, busy as I am
trying to calculate a way back to you
that doesn't require turnpike exits.

2.

Another day goes to voicemail.
I play 'Chicken' with myself
until I wake unemployed
in a Super 8. I spend whole afternoons
sunbathing on railroad tracks.
These risks are necessary.
I must get to the palsied last breath
of a closeout sale. The crustaceans
are cheapest in recession. For you,
I'll admit it. My long lost
coupon hoarder, I still hope to find
you in that place where my warranties
finally void.

3.

The lease ends
so I squat in my own heart,
spend the rest of my days dreaming
of lost teeth. I am shallower
than a puddle-drunk cricket.
I needed this grief to realize
there's no romance in singing
with your knees, with the body's yielding.
What has love ever done anyway
besides crash my last Honda Civic?
I want to learn instead from the seafloor,
where the crabs replace their departed wives
with rocks. It is dark down there, after all.
Who will tell the difference?

4.

The prom is not saved.
You are defeated by your sadness
in a sports stadium named after
cheap auto-insurance policies.
I remain a drug-addicted
shoe salesman and the stars
are a long distance from me here
in China, Maine. Let the losses pile
like waves, like seals virused
and glittering on a shore:
so we were promised love,
so the liver is a sledgehammer,
so this austerity will never end,
so what? We can bleed endlessly.
We are jellyfish, our blood
only jelly, and we'll never
fall for a disguise again, because
everyone should know everyone else
is fake and a face is nothing
more than the light Velcroed to it.
At the bar I send back my beer.
There are better ways
to be hammered, better ways
of becoming the nail.

ESCAPE FROM THE INTERGALACTIC LUNAR PRISON

Four suns hang in an alien sky.
Suddenly it's Thursday
and as if I hadn't surrendered enough this week
I go to the bar. Obviously my nemesis
there thwarts me at karaoke, seals me
forever in the intergalactic lunar prison.
So I learn to meditate, to long
for myself so completely I vanish.
This whole town weighs less
than a bird's heartbeat anyway:
no one will care what the snow plows carve
on the wrong side of the moon.

MECHA GODZILLA LOVE POEM

When I think of you, I'm actually
thinking of a distillation of organs.
Livers, kidneys, vessels
through which blood flows
like the dappled leaf shadows
whose shifting I never saw
because I spent my summers alone
in basements wondering if bugs
have hearts or even lungs.
No one knows. God is dead.
Society crumbled so we built
a giant robot and launched that baby
to space to do battle with a species
of cricket-sized aliens, because
we need triumphs now more than ever,
no matter how small and scurrying they may be.
It's like this morning when I took
a beer instead of Tylenol, vanquished
a whole day before it even started.
To the liver it's all the same,
mere surges in the gut, and in fact

I often mistake bowel quivers for love
and you my lover for your evil clone.
Because what is a robot anyway
but an overgrown insect? What is
a heart except a collapsing colony.
What are you if not the shore
upon which I may finally crash,
take stock of myself, and formulate
a world worth worshipping.

Acknowledgements

Grateful acknowledgment to the following publications where some of these poems have previously appeared: *Neutral Spaces Magazine, Back Patio Press, The Staten Islander, Joyless House, Forever Magazine, Fluland, Vanity Press, Grody Mag, The Quaranzine, Misery Tourism, Gay Death Trance, DFL Lit, Philosophical Idiot, Tragickal,* and *Heaven Map.*

Immense thanks as well for the support from GG 'Cowboy' Roland, Zac Smith, Cavin Bryce Gonzalez, Giacomo Pope, Mike Andrelczyk, Troy James Weaver, Furnitureman, 'Luigi', AEC, all the people who DM'd me medical advice on Twitter when I thought there was something wrong with my scrotum, Richie, Mackenzie, Neal, Madellyne, my cats, and, most importantly, my girlfriend.

Nathaniel Duggan is a former mattress salesman. He lives in Maine.

Also available from Back Patio Press...

Poetry
Sad Sad Boy by Michael O'Brien

Liver Mush by Graham Irvin

Watertown by Dan Eastman

Novels
Good at Drugs by KKUURRTT

Numbskull by No Glykon

Venice by T. J. Larkey

Photographs of Madness by Alec Ivan Fugate

Short Fiction
Time. Wow. by Neil Clark

Printed in Great Britain
by Amazon

28130438R00056